Thrifting and Flipping Vintage Toys & Dolls

By Amanda Symonds

Table of Contents

What is vintage toy flipping?

Vintage toy flipping is a popular and profitable business that involves buying vintage toys at low prices, restoring them, and reselling them for a higher price. As an expert in this field, I know all the ins and outs of vintage toy flipping, from finding the best deals to negotiating with buyers.

Whether you're looking to flip vintage Strawberry Shortcake dolls, Barbies or vintage Transformers, there are many tips and strategies that can help you be successful in this lucrative business. Some key things to keep in mind when flipping vintage toys include knowing your market well, choosing high-quality pieces, investing in quality restoration tools and supplies, and building strong relationships with potential buyers.

With the right knowledge and skills, you can make a good living flipping vintage toys and turning a profit on your investment.

How to start vintage toy flipping

If you're interested in vintage toy flipping, the first step is to research and find out what types of vintage toys are selling well in your market. You may also want to consider investing in high-quality restoration tools and supplies so that you can turn vintage toys into beautiful pieces that buyers will be eager to purchase.

Once you have found a few sources, you need to be able to spot a good deal and negotiate effectively with vintage toy sellers. You need to research what you are buying, how easy it will be to resell and what the expected sale price might be.

Finally, it's important to have a good understanding of the market and know how to sell your vintage toys for top dollar. This may involve using online platforms like eBay or social media sites like Instagram and Facebook, as well as attending vintage toy conventions or flea markets in person.

Setting a budget and taking on the right mindset are also key to success in vintage toy flipping. You need to be prepared to make some initial investments, such as buying vintage toys at a low price and investing in quality restoration tools and supplies. Additionally, you should focus on joining a few Facebook groups for collectors to build up some rapport.

With the right knowledge, skills, and strategies, you can be successful flipping vintage toys for profit!

Thrifting tips

Thrifting is more than just a hobby – it can be a great way to make some extra money on the side. Whether you're buying and selling clothes, furniture, or other items, there are plenty of ways to turn your thrifting skills into a profitable business.

Only buy what you think you can resell for a profit. When you thrift you need to use your smart phone to take photos using the Google Lens and have it set to Shopping so it will identify and value your items as you pick them up. This is a quick way to identify rare collectables and see current prices online. You may need to check eBay.com to see if they sell easily, otherwise it is a great tool to help you know what to spend and weed out the trash from the treasure in the store.

One of the most important things to keep in mind when starting a thrifting business is to focus on items in high demand. This means researching what types of products people are buying, and looking for those products at thrift stores, yard sales, and other places where you can find good deals. You may also want to consider partnering with other local businesses or resellers in order to get access to a wider variety of items.

If you partner with another reseller and they are looking for vintage cars, then they can send you a photo if they find vintage dolls etc. You can get them to buy things if they are $5 and then reimburse them later when you collect your items. It can be great, if you trust their judgement and agree on some basic rules together.

Another key to success as a thrifter is to be organized and efficient. This means keeping detailed records of your sales, so that you can track trends and make the most of your business opportunities. It also means developing systems for sorting through and managing the various items you come across, so that you don't waste time and effort on things that aren't worth your time or money.

While thrifting involves some risk, with the right approach it can be a great way to make extra cash and build your own business empire. So if you're ready to start making some serious money through thrifting, get out there and start hunting for those high-demand items!

How to ensure a profit

1. you "add value" via repair, cleaning, restoration (e.g., buying broken dolls or toys cheap and fixing them). I'd polish them, replace bad crystals, put on new straps, and sell them right back on eBay. You need to be given the right tools and skills or hire someone who has them.

or

2. arbitrage (e.g., buying low in one region and selling high elsewhere).

or

3. random good luck (e.g., finding something cheap at a thrift or pawn shop or listed incorrectly on eBay)

4. selling on an exclusive website or store that charges full price for rare collectables in perfect condition.

Odd and unusual vintage items sell well

I had planned to mainly talk about vintage dolls and toys in this book. However, there is no shortage of unusual items that sell well online, from rare antiques and vintage collectibles to quirky novelty items and one-of-a-kind handmade goods.

Some popular items include handcrafted jewelry made from unexpected materials, art prints and posters with unique designs or vintage themes, and kitschy home decor pieces that showcase a fun and quirky sense of style. Other popular categories include music memorabilia such as vinyl records, movie posters and other film-related merchandise, and rare collectible toys.

Another category of item that frequently sells well online is rare books, particularly those with limited editions or signed copies. With the right marketing strategy, you can reach a wide audience of book collectors and enthusiasts who are looking for these types of unique items.

To succeed as an online seller of unusual items, it is essential to build a strong online presence and develop relationships with your customers. This can involve using social media platforms such as Facebook and Instagram to share photos of your products and engage with potential buyers by creating a website or blog that highlights your unique offerings.

You should also be prepared to respond quickly to customer inquiries, address any issues with products promptly, and provide exceptional service in order to build a loyal following of repeat buyers. With the right approach, you can turn your love for odd and unusual items into a profitable business venture.

My parents had several antique shops over decades, and I learnt that the story that you tell about your collectable item and the way it is presented determines the price the item is worth in the buyer's mind. If you can tell a good story then you can get a great price!

If you can establish a connection to a famous person or important event then you can command a higher price too. This applies to in-person sales and online auctions as well.

BARGAIN BUYING

Let's look at one example in detail, Strawberry Shortcake Dolls.

How to buy a 1980s collectable doll

Strawberry Shortcake Dolls are becoming increasingly popular as more and more people appreciate the quality and craftsmanship that goes into these pieces. If you're thinking of investing in a collectable doll, it's important to be aware of the going rates for different dolls.

In this guide, we'll provide pricing information for collectable dolls. With this information, you'll be able to shop with confidence and find the perfect doll dolls for your needs. Let's get started!

What to look for when buying a second hand doll

When shopping for collectable dolls, there are a few things you'll want to keep in mind.

1. Consider the condition of the piece.

2. Consider rarity and demand for the doll / collectable.

3. Consider your budget. Some collectable dolls can be expensive, but most are cheaper so you will find plenty of budget-friendly options if you know where to look.

Keep in mind that prices may vary depending on the condition of the doll and the seller.

How to determine the value of a collectable

A good place to begin your search for the ideal collectable is with the information provided in this guide

When choosing a collectable, it is important first to find the toy that is popular and will make money on resale and then evaluate the specific toy's condition before making a final decision on price.

This guide is divided into three sections:

- Various price points

- Checklist for Adjusting Prices

- Tips for determining prices

Grading items

The first time you look for collectables, you'll notice a wide variety of dolls/toys at varying prices. Determining the condition of the collectable is also called 'grading'. You might feel quite intimidated by it all! No worries - we'll give you the information you will need to sort it all out.

- Choose the collectable you're interested in. This will reduce the number of item you need to consider and help you learn all about that particular item. You can use your smartphone to take photos using the Google Lens and have it set to Shopping so it will identify and value your items as you pick them up. This is a quick way to identify rare collectables and see current prices online.

- As soon as you have a solid understanding of that one item, you can decide how much you want to pay.

- Determine what price you are willing to pay for it. You will need to decide on the condition, your ability, and how much effort you would like to put into restoring the collectable, as well as where you will look for it. You'll need to consider all of these factors when you're deciding what price to pay.

SEE APPENDIX FOR PRICE TABLE

Checklist for Adjusting Prices

Now that you've decided on the item and what you're willing to pay, it's time to get into the nitty-gritty of it all - the actual prices.

Here is a checklist of items to keep in mind when evaluating a doll:

1. The model number

2. The age of the doll

3. The condition of the doll

4. The completeness of the doll (accessories, original box etc)

5. Any restoration that has been done to the doll

6. Re-issues are not as valuable as original vintage dolls

It's possible to buy a lot of extra pieces for your doll online, but you'll have to do your research and pay for them, which can be pricey depending on what you need and how old your doll is.

Factors that influence the price

The following factors can impact the price of collectable dolls:

- The condition of the doll

- Whether or not the doll is complete

- The age of the doll

- The rarity of the doll

- The desirability of the doll

It is sad to say that the highest price goes to the toys that have never been taken out of the box (or played with). Keep these things in mind when considering the price of a collectable!

Where to find vintage toys for sale

Prices for Strawberry Shortcake Dolls vary depending on the doll's condition and rarity. However, as a general rule of thumb, prices for Strawberry Shortcake Dolls start at around $20 and can go up to $300 or more for rare dolls.

There are a few different places you can look for collectables for sale. Here are a few of the most popular:

- Thrift shops in your area

- eBay

- Local Antique stores

- Online classified ads (Facebook Marketplace, eBay, Craigslist, Kijiji)

- Garage sales

- Local newspaper

- Flea Markets

- Pawnshop

- Antique Shops

When you are looking for collectable dolls, keep in mind that you should inspect the doll before purchasing it. Make sure to check for things like missing clothes and damage.

8 Tips for negotiating the price

If you find a collectable doll or toy that you are interested in but the asking price is too high, don't be afraid to negotiate.

Here are a few tips to help you get the best deal possible:

1. Do your research ahead of time and know how much the item is worth. Look at our tables in the Appendix. This will give you a good starting point for negotiating.

2. Be polite and respectful when negotiating. The seller is more likely to be willing to negotiate if they feel like you are a reasonable person.

3. Be realistic about what you're willing to pay for a doll. If the seller doesn't budge on the price, then it's probably not worth your time and money to buy the doll.

4. Know what the item is worth. Do your research before you go to buy it.

5. If you're buying a collectable from an individual, try to find out how much they paid for it. This will help in negotiations.

6. Offer a lower price than what you're actually willing to pay. This might make the seller more willing to work with you.

7. If the seller has several dolls or toys for sale, they might be more willing to lower the price on one item in order to make a sale.

8. Don't be afraid to walk away from a deal if the price is too high. There are plenty of other collectables out there, so don't feel rushed into making a purchase.

With these tips in mind, you should be able to get a great deal on a collectable doll.

Other questions to ask the seller

- Can I inspect the doll or toy (if local)?

- Are there any other accessories included that are not in the photos?

- Is there an original box?

- Can you deliver the doll to me? What is the estimated shipping cost? Insurance?

- Why are you selling the doll?

- Questions about the condition

- Have you had any other offers recently? If no, this can lead to you asking if the price negotiable?

Selling FAQ's

Q: What is the average price for collectable dolls?

A: As a general rule of thumb, prices for Strawberry Shortcake Dolls start at around $20 and can go up to $300 or more for rare dolls.

Let's look at selling next.

How to sell your collectable dolls or toys

Selling your collectables can seem like a daunting task. But with a little research and elbow grease, you can get top dollar for your thrifted doll or toy.

In this section, we'll walk you through the entire process of selling your doll or collection. First, we'll help you determine its value. Then, we'll show you how to market it effectively. Finally, we'll outline the steps you need to take to complete the sale. So, whether you're looking to sell for cash or just want to find a new home for it, this guide has you covered!

By following our tips, you can ensure that your retro collectable dolls sell quickly and for a fair price. We know that selling your old collectable dolls can be a daunting task, but with our advice, it can be much easier and stress-free!

Determining the value of your collectable

The first step in selling your doll is determining its value. There are a few factors you'll need to consider, such as age, condition, brand, and features. Here's a quick overview of each:

1. Age: Generally speaking, the older and rarer your Strawberry Shortcake Dolls are, the more valuable they will be.

2. Condition: A doll in good condition will fetch a higher price than one that's in poor condition.

3. Brand: Some brands of dolls are more sought-after than others.

4. Features: Certain features can add value to your doll

5. Check whether it makes sense to include two items together or separate different dolls. Don't separate a doll and its pet.

Ways to add value to your piece of vintage toy flipping: Make sure you have the original box! This is crucial to get the highest price. It is sad to say that the highest price goes to the toys that have never been taken out of the box (or played with).

Once you've considered all of these factors, it's time to do some research.

- Online Auctions: Sites like Facebook Marketplace, eBay and Etsy are great places to start your research. Simply type in the make and model of your doll to get an idea of its value.

- Antique Stores: If you have any local antique dealers, they may be able to give you an estimate of your doll's value.

- Appraisers: You can also hire an appraiser to give you a professional opinion of your doll's worth.

After you've done your research, you should have a good idea of how much your doll is worth. From there, you can start to market it effectively!

The five stages to selling your collectables

- Research: Determine the value of your doll or toy and research what it's worth.

- Getting Ready: Clean and polish your doll or toy, and make sure it's in good condition.

- Advertising: Advertise your doll/toy online or in local stores/classifieds.

- Closing the Deal: Complete the sale and hand it over or ship your doll to its new owner.

- Shipping: Pack your doll carefully to avoid damage during shipping. Purchase insurance if the sale is over $100.

Now that you know the steps involved in selling your collectable, let's take a closer look at each one.

1. Research

Researching the value of your doll/toy is crucial. As we mentioned earlier, you'll need to consider factors such as age, condition, brand, and features.

The condition and worth of your equipment will help you choose a price and give you an idea of how simple it will be to sell. If it is an antique and in excellent condition, it will be much easier to sell than if it's a newer item in poor condition.

Once you've determined how, when and where to sell your product it's time for one last step. This is the most important part because without an appropriate price point everything else will be useless! Research prices in nearby areas so that potential customers can find out if they're getting a good deal or not based on what others are charging locally- this way no matter where someone lives there'll always be some form of competition that forces down costs across all regions.

2. Getting ready

Preparation is essential after you have chosen to sell a doll. If you haven't already, I strongly suggest cleaning and repairing the doll. A refurbished doll always looks better than a dirty, old one. If everything is in order, take pictures of your doll from all angles and write an ad that will catch someone's eye.

Here is another example, getting a Strawberry Shortcake Doll ready for sale.

Preparing your item for sale

Preparing your doll might take a day to do correctly. Don't forget their outfits either; if there are any stains they need to be carefully spot washed to remove them.

If you decide to iron their clothes, it might be better to cover them with a tea towel first and try the lowest setting. You don't want to damage their vintage clothes. This makeover might be just what she needs to make her look her best!

Don't forget to brush her hair and don't panic if it is matted- as any tangled tresses are less important when your Strawberry Shortcake character doll is wearing a hat.

Remove musty or smoky smells from dolls

Give the dolls somewhere to air for a few days. This should undercover and not in a place where they can get wet from rain etc.

Put the doll into a closed plastic container with baking soda or new kitty litter to absorb the smell. Putting them on top of a cloth, placed in a new kitty litter tray could do the trick.

Don't attempt to use Febreeze to mask the smell if you plan to sell the doll. Some people find it off putting, just like a musty or smoky smell.

If you are posting the doll, keep in mind that smells can intensify when shipped in bubblewrap and the first whiff could be very strong. After that the smell will diminish.

Some people carefully wash doll clothes and try to remove stains by handwashing in cold water.

Cleaning your doll's pet

Does your Strawberry Shortcake doll have a pet? You should clean it with dishwashing detergent and an old toothbrush to get rid of grubby marks.

Obtaining the best price for your doll

What do I need to remember to sell vintage Strawberry Shortcake dolls for the top price?

Most collectors want dolls in their original boxes, preferably unopened. Having a squashed box with your doll is better than no box. Also look to see that you have located the doll's tights, shoes, combs, perfume and pets etc. You need to have a complete set to get the best price.

You might want to freshen up the appearance of your Strawberry Shortcake doll by spraying a little bit of perfume on your doll. We have written a perfume guide about which perfume which matches the doll's original scent here.

Selling checklist

With a clear sense of what you want your final price point to be, take this simple checklist below before listing anything online.

-Have a complete description of the item with all relevant features (the below pictures may also help)

-Clean product getting ready for sale (worth noting they'll sometimes reject sales because it was incompletely depicted)

-Categorize your auction appropriately or suffer from decreased visibility in search results

Where can I sell Strawberry Shortcake dolls for the top price?

It really depends on what you're looking for. If it's a high-value doll then eBay might be the best option because they offer a number of different categories where people are looking for Strawberry Shortcake Dolls. The downside with this site is that items do not sell right away so there's no telling how long it will take before someone decides to buy yours. But, If you want to get rid of your doll as soon as possible Poshmark might be perfect – but again, I'm not sure whether or not they have good prices! It would all come down to personal preference and what kind of price range you're willing to go to.

The best thing to do would be to post yours on several sites and see what happens – but if you're looking for a quick sale I suggest the latter!

How can I check whether I have a complete and genuine Strawberry Shortcake doll?

These dolls were produced by Kenner from 1980-1987, they are based on American Greetings' animated cartoon series Strawberry shortcake and her friends that aired in 1981-1983. The doll was first introduced with pink hair ribbons as well as yellow flower dresses; later releases featured more outfits than before. You can check your doll against the pictures of other sellers and know for sure where are the markings are for different dolls and what outfits and pets came with your doll.

3. Advertising

Now it's time to advertise your items. You have a few
options:

- Internet Ads (Facebook Marketplace, eBay,
  Craigslist, Poshmark, Kijiji)

- Local newspaper

- Flea Markets

- Antique Shops (on consignment)

Each method of advertising will have its own unique
benefits and drawbacks. For example, placing an ad in
the local paper is great if you want to sell quickly, but
you may not get as much money for your doll. Selling at
a flea market is great if you want to make some quick
cash, but it's not always the best place to find serious
buyers who want to give you a decent price for your
doll.

You can sell directly to a pawnshop or dealer and they
will on-sell your doll. Your local antique or collectables

shop may also be interested in purchasing it (or selling it on consignment) so it doesn't hurt to ask. You can also sell a broken doll for clothes, accessories etc.

The best way to sell your doll is by placing an ad online. By doing this, you can reach a large audience of potential buyers. Be sure to take good quality pictures of your doll and write a detailed description. You should also research and set a fair price for your doll.

When selling online, the best way to reach potential buyers is through the internet. By placing an ad on eBay, Craigslist, Poshmark or Kijiji, you can reach a large audience of potential buyers. Some of these ads also have the added benefit of being free to post!

Poshmark: This app has been gaining popularity over the years and more than likely if you're reading this article then Poshmark might be a good bet too! They allow listings up to $100, which makes them perfect for selling those high-quality items – I haven't used this app before so I am not sure whether it gets reasonable prices or not.

If you decide to sell your doll online, there are a few things you should keep in mind. First, take some good quality pictures of your doll. Be sure to include close-ups of any interesting features or damage.

Finally, set a fair price for your doll and accept offers from interested buyer including estimated postage costs. If you need a trailer to transport the doll, best to mention this in the ad too!

Marketing your doll or toy online

Now that you know how much your doll is worth, it's time to start marketing it! The best way to do this is by creating a listing on online auction sites or classified websites.

Here are a few tips to help you get started:

1. Be Honest: When describing your doll, be honest about its condition. Don't try to hide any flaws, as this will only lead to disappointment for the buyer.

2. Include Pictures: A picture is worth a thousand words, so be sure to include plenty of pictures of your doll.

3. Price It Right: Don't overprice your doll, as this will likely scare buyers away. Try to price it at around market value.

4. Be Patient: It may take a while for your doll to sell, so be patient and keep it listed until you find the right buyer.

5. Selling Your Doll

6. Once you've found a buyer, it's time to finalize the sale. This process will vary depending on the method of payment you've chosen. For example, if you're selling locally, you may opt to accept cash or a check. If you're selling online, you'll likely need to meet the buyer or ship the doll to the buyer.

If you're selling your doll online, there are a few things to keep in mind.

1. First, take clear, well-lit photos of your doll from all angles. Be sure to include any accessories that come with the doll, such as a carrying case or extra feet.

2. Next, write a clear and concise description of your doll, including all the important details potential buyers will want to know. Be honest about the condition of the doll, and be sure to mention any damage or wear.

3. Finally, set a fair and reasonable price for your doll. Be sure to do your research before setting a price, and be prepared to negotiate with potential buyers.

With these tips from the experts, you'll be able to sell your collectable quickly and easily - and get the best price possible.

Here are a few tips to help you finalize the sale:

- Get Insurance: If you're shipping your doll, be sure to get insurance. This will protect your investment in case the doll is damaged during shipping.

- Pack It Properly: When packing your doll, be sure to use plenty of bubble wrap and packing peanuts. This will help ensure that it arrives safely at its destination.

- Stay Safe: If you're selling locally, be sure to tell a neighbour or friend you are having people come to your home. If you not keen to have people to your home, then consider meeting in a public place and bring a friend along if you are not confident. This will help ensure your safety during the transaction.

By following these tips, you can sell your doll quickly and easily!

Here are great 1980s doll listings from eBay.com

The best examples for Strawberry Shortcake dolls I have seen are from the seller auntieandisattic and she did an excellent job.

Peach Blush with Trellis Deluxe Mini

Condition: Used
Ended: Mar 08, 2022, 1:07PM

Winning bid: **US $2,257.00** [8 bids]

Vintage Strawberry Shortcake Baby NEEDS A NAME Doll Blows Kisses NIB

★ ★ ★ ★ ★ 1 product rating | Write a review

Condition: New

Sold for: **US $105.00**

No interest if paid in full in 6
mo on $99+*

Shipping: $51.29 International Priority Shipping to Australia via the Global
Shipping Program @ | See details
Located in: Waynesville, North Carolina, United States

Delivery: Estimated within 27-33 business days @
Includes international tracking

Returns: Seller does not accept returns | See details

Payments: PayPal | G Pay | VISA | ● | ● | ● |

PayPal CREDIT
*No interest if paid in full in 6 months on $99+. | See terms and apply now

Any international shipping and import charges are paid in part to Pitney Bowes Inc.
Learn More

Vintage 1980s Strawberry Shortcake Berry / Berrykin Princess

Condition: New

Sold for: **US $259.99**

No interest if paid in full in 6
mo on $99+*

Shipping: $36.23 International Priority Shipping to Australia via the Global
Shipping Program @ | See details
Located in: Shawnee, Kansas, United States

Delivery: Estimated within 27-33 business days @
Includes international tracking

Returns: Seller does not accept returns | See details

Payments: PayPal | G Pay | VISA | ● | ● | ● |

PayPal CREDIT
*No interest if paid in full in 6 months on $99+. | See terms and apply now

Any international shipping and import charges are paid in part to Pitney Bowes Inc.
Learn More

strawberry Shortcake cookie jar

Condition: Used
"American Greetings Strawberry Shortcake Cookie Jar"

Sold for: **US $400.00**

$36 for 12 months with
PayPal Credit*

Shipping: May not ship to Australia - Read item description or contact seller
for shipping options. | See details
Located in: Anchorage, Alaska, United States

Delivery: Varies

Returns: Seller does not accept returns | See details

Payments: PayPal G Pay VISA

PayPal CREDIT

*$36 for 12 months. Minimum purchase required. | See terms and apply now

Vintage Strawberry Shortcake Minis with Case

Condition: Used

Sold for: **US $190.00**

No Interest if paid in full in 6
mo on $99+*

Shipping: May not ship to Australia - Read item description or contact seller
for shipping options. | See details
Located in: New York, New York, United States

Delivery: Varies

Returns: Seller does not accept returns | See details

Payments: PayPal G Pay VISA

PayPal CREDIT

*No Interest if paid in full in 6 months on $99+. | See terms and apply now

4. Closing the deal

It's always a good idea to test the item before you sell it. This will help to ensure that there are no problems with it and that it is in good condition. (If it is in a sealed box when ignore this advice).

When the buyer receives the collectable, you could include a receipt or some other form of proof of purchase. If all goes well, you will have successfully sold your item and can now enjoy the extra cash!

5. Shipping

Once you have found a buyer, and they are local then you don't need to worry about this.

The most important thing to remember when shipping a doll is to pack it securely. Use plenty of packing peanuts or bubble wrap to protect the item from damage during transit. It's also a good idea to use a sturdy box that will not easily collapse.

I would recommend checking out local companies that may be able to pack and ship the box for you and you would need to measure the doll and know the length and weight in advance in order to get a shipping quote (to tell the buyer). Finally, be sure to include shipping insurance. This will help protect you in case the item is damaged during transit.

The entire process of selling a collectable can be completed in four stages: consideration, preparation, advertisement, and sale. By keeping these simple tips in mind, you'll be able to successfully sell your items with little effort!

Online selling FAQs

Q: How do I know if the buyer is serious?

A: If the buyer is asking lots of questions about the doll and seems genuinely interested, they are probably a serious buyer. If they say they are looking for a particular doll to complete their collection, then they are more likely to be a good buyer.

Q: What if the buyer wants to pay by check?

A: Take only cash, if possible, to avoid any potential problems with bounced checks. Paypal is another option but you need to sign up for an account in advance.

Q. Should you offer a return policy on any collectables?

A. No, I wouldn't. It is up to you.

Tips for avoiding scams when selling collectibles

Collecting is a fun and interesting hobby that can be turned into a profitable business. However, it's important to be aware of the many scams that are out there so you don't get taken advantage of. In this section, we will discuss our tips for avoiding scams when selling collectibles. Follow these tips and you'll be able to sell your items with confidence!

• Do your research. It's important to have a good understanding of what you're selling before you enter into any transaction. Know the value of your item and don't be afraid to walk away if someone is offering you far less than it's worth.

• Be aware of common scams. There are many different scams that collectors need to be aware of, such as fake items being offered for sale, or sellers who refuse to ship items after payment has been made. If you're unsure about a particular transaction, it's always best to err on the side of caution and walk away.

- Use reputable sources where possible. When buying or selling collectibles, always use reputable sources. This includes online auction sites, dealer websites, and forums. Avoid buying from individuals who you don't know and can't verify as being legitimate. If they are a new seller account on eBay with no feedback, don't buy it! If it sounds too good to be true, it often is. If you can afford to lose the money on a very rare collectable then weight up the risks before you do it.

- Pay attention to red flags. There are some red flags that should always send up a warning signal when you're dealing with collectibles. These include sellers who are unwilling to provide photos of the item, or who refuse to answer questions about the item. If you see any red flags, walk away from the deal.

- Insist on getting details in writing. Any time you're entering into a transaction for a collectible, make sure that there is a written string of messages in place. This includes things like shipping costs, payment methods, and return policies. This will help to avoid any misunderstandings later on. This will protect both you and the other party in case of any problems and you can use the conversation if you have to provide proof to eBay or Amazon about the transaction.

- Use escrow services (escrow.com) above $500. If possible, always use an escrow service when buying or selling collectibles. This will protect you if the other party doesn't hold up their end of the deal.

- Insure your items. When shipping collectibles over $150, always insure the items for their full value. Some carriers offer insurance up to a certain value. This will protect you in case the items are lost or damaged in transit.

- Track your shipments. Always keep a tracking number for any shipments you send out. This will help you to locate the shipment if it's lost, and will also give you proof that you sent the item if there are any problems with the delivery. Some people say the delivery never arrived when it did!

- Be patient. Selling collectibles can be a slow process, so it's important to be patient. Don't be rushed into any deals, and take the time to find the right buyer for your items. By following these tips, you'll be able to avoid scams and sell your collectibles with confidence!

Becoming a Licensed Secondhand Dealer

If you're looking for a new flipping business opportunity, becoming a licensed secondhand dealer may be the perfect choice for you! This is a rapidly growing industry, and there are many opportunities for entrepreneurs who are willing to put in the hard work.

There are many benefits to becoming a licensed secondhand dealer. One of the biggest advantages is that you will have access to a large number of potential customers. Secondhand dealers are able to sell their products to anyone who is interested, which means that there is a much larger market for your goods.

Additionally, becoming a licensed secondhand dealer also allows you to operate your business without having to worry about certain regulations that apply to other types of businesses.

If you're thinking about becoming a licensed secondhand dealer, there are a few things you should keep in mind.

First, it's important to research the laws in your state or country so that you are familiar with the regulations surrounding this type of business.

Additionally, it's always a good idea to build up a strong network of contacts in the industry. This will help you find the best deals on products and also give you access to potential customers.

Finally, remember that becoming a licensed secondhand dealer is a big commitment - be sure that you are ready to put in the time and effort required to make your business successful.

In conclusion, becoming licensed secondhand dealer has many benefits including a large number of potential customers, not having to worry about certain regulations, and building a strong network. If you are thinking about becoming licensed, remember to research the laws, build up a network of contacts, and be prepared to put in time and effort to make your business successful.

Custom toy modding: the ultimate guide

Collectors all around the world want to modify their collections to make them unique and one of a kind. Whether it's painting a toy car in their favorite color or adding new accessories to a figurine, customizing toys is a fun way to show off your personality and style. In this guide, we will teach you everything you need to know about custom toy modding!

Custom toy modding is a fun and creative way to express yourself while showing off your creativity and ingenuity. You can then charge top prices for your unique pieces!

Whether you are modifying a car, action figure, or figurine, there are endless possibilities when it comes to customizing toys! In this guide, we will cover the basics of custom toy modding, including tools and materials needed for customizing and the different techniques you can use to create your own unique creations. We will also talk about where to find inspiration for custom toy mods, as well as how to take care of your toys once they have been customized. So if you're ready to get started on your very own custom toy mod, keep reading!

What is Custom Toy Modding?

Custom toy modding is the process of transforming a standard toy into something completely unique and one of a kind. Whether it is painting, adding accessories or modifying the design, there are countless ways to customize toys! Some popular methods for customizing toys include painting, repainting, adding stickers or decals, altering the shape or design with tools like scissors or wire cutters, or even using 3D printers to create new parts from scratch.

The Tools and Materials You Need for Custom Toy Modding

Before you can start customizing toys, you will need a few basic supplies and materials. The exact tools and materials needed will depend on what type of customization you want to do - for example, if you want to repaint a toy car, you will need paint brushes and paints. But there are some basic tools and materials that you will need no matter what type of customizing you do. These include:

• Scissors or wire cutters - for altering the shape or design of the toys

• Paint brushes or sponges - for painting or repainting toys

• A variety of paints, including acrylics, enamels, urethanes, lacquers, and inks - these can be used to paint different surfaces like plastic, metal, rubber, fabric and more! Choose paints that are best suited for your specific project. For example, if you are working with plastic toys, you will want to use paints that are specifically designed for plastic surfaces.

• A variety of stickers, decals, and other adhesives - these can be used to add designs or accessories to your toys.

• Modification equipment like sandpaper, wire, tape, glue guns and more - depending on what you are trying to do with your toys, you may need one or all of these different types of modification tools!

It is also important to choose the right type of surface for your customizing project. Different materials require different painting methods and adhesives. For example, if you are customizing a toy car made from synthetic rubber (synthetic polymer), then you will want to use paints that are specifically designed for synthetic surfaces, as using regular paints may cause the paint to crack or peel.

Tips for Finding Inspiration for Custom Toy Mods

One of the best things about customizing toys is that you can create anything your imagination can come up with! This means that there are endless possibilities when it comes to finding inspiration for your mods. Some popular sources of toy modding inspiration include pop culture, video games, comics and cartoons, music and celebrities. You can also get ideas from Pinterest using everyday objects like flowers, animals, cars, kitchen utensils - whatever inspires you! If you need some help getting started on your own custom toy projects, try browsing online forums or DIY blogs for ideas and tips from other customizers. There are also many online tutorials, ebooks and books that can help you learn new techniques for customizing toys.

How to Take Care of Your Custom Toys

Once your toy mods are complete, it is important to take good care of them so they will last as long as possible. This means storing your toys properly and cleaning them on a regular basis! When storing your toys, do not place heavy objects or other items on top of them. If the surface is rough or uneven, this may cause scratches or damage to the paint or design. Keeping your toys in a cool, dry place will also help prolong their life.

Cleaning your toys is important because it helps prevent dust and dirt from building up on the surface. Dust can cause paint to chip or peel, so be sure to clean your toys at least once every few months using a soft cloth and non-abrasive cleaning products like soap and water. After you have finished customizing a toy, keep it in a cool place away from direct sunlight until you are ready to display it!

By following these tips for customizing toys, you will be able to create one-of-a-kind mods that are unique and beautiful. Whether you want to repaint an old dollhouse or turn action figures into zombies, there is no limit when it comes to fun. I would start working on broken toys for practise and then grow your modding business from there.

What expenses are involved in a toy business?

There are many different expenses involved in running a vintage toy flipping business. Some of the main ones include buying vintage toys at low prices, purchasing quality restoration tools and supplies, and paying for things like advertising and marketing to reach potential buyers. Additionally, you may need to set aside money for taxes, business licenses, or other fees depending on your location and type of business.

Doll repair tools you may need

When getting started in vintage toy flipping, you will likely need to invest in a wide range of tools and supplies for restoring vintage dolls. Some of the most essential items are the same as those used for modding and include paints, brushes, glues, clippers and pliers, sanding paper, and other basic repair equipment. Additionally, it may be helpful to have specialized doll-specific tools like needle nose pliers or doll stands for displaying products. With the right tools on hand, you can successfully restore vintage toys and sell them at top dollar!

Toy repair tools you may need

When flipping vintage metal cars, there are a variety of tools and supplies you may need to invest in. Some of the most essential items are the same as those used for modding and include metal clippers and pliers for removing dents and scratches, paints, glues, sanding paper or other abrasives for restoring paintwork, and basic tools like wrenches for tightening screws or bolts. Additionally, you may want to consider investing in specialized car repair tools like tire irons or oil drip pans. With these tools on hand, you can successfully flip or mod metal cars and make a profit!

Conclusion

Whether you are a seasoned vintage doll or toy collector or just getting started, there are many different strategies and techniques that can help you succeed in this exciting and profitable business. Whether it's investing in high-quality restoration tools and supplies, building up your network of collectors and buyers, or negotiating with confidence, there are many ways to add value to your vintage toy flipping business. Building relationships with licensed second-hand dealers will help you enormously.

With our tips, you'll be sure to make a quick and easy sale - and get the best price possible. We hope that you found our guide helpful and that your doll or toy collection sells quickly and for a fair price.

Please remember to leave a review so others can find our book.

Appendix

This is a selective list of only what has been sold on ebay.com in March 2022

US ebay prices current March 2022		
Item	**Price estimate (US$)**	
Kenner original (has box)	30-67	1979
Lime Chiffon, Cherry Cuddler, Butter Cookie, Angel Cake, and Sour Grapes	50	1981
Almond Tea Doll & Pet Marza Panda 1980's with Box	80	1983
Berrykins Dolls		
Berrykin Banana Twirl And Critter (no box)	725	1984
Berrykin Banana Twirl (no box)	210	1984
Orange blossom and critter	500	
Mint Tulip and from Mint Tulip Berrykin	717	1985
Berrykin Re-issues in box. Some marked EU collection	60-80	

Berry Princess (in box)	260	1980s
Berry Bake Shoppe in box	90-124	1980
Baby Strawberry Shortcake Blow-a-Kiss Doll	200	
Peach Blush with Trellis Deluxe Mini	2257	
Vintage Strawberry Shortcake Minis with Case	190	
Strawberry Shortcake Cookie Jar	400	
Fun Room Furniture Toy Box Chest	275	
Fun Room Furniture Record player	309	
Furniture Fun Room Piano and Stool	385	
Fun Room Furniture ATTIC FURNITURE 5 piece Set	225	
Plush Pets	85	
Almond Tea on Cushion mini	57	
Huckleberry Pie 16" Vinyl Headed Rag Dolls	110	1980s
Vintage Strawberry Shortcake Vinyl Head Rag Doll	79	
Peach Blush Getting Ready For Bed Mini Sealed	165	
Cherry Cuddler With Gooseberry Mini 1984 Sealed	140	
Mini Prototype First Shot Sample Rare Vintage 1984	85	1984
Mint Tulip Marsh Mallard shoe mini miniature without box	80	1984

US ebay prices current March 2022	
Model	**Price estimate (US$)**
Strawberry Shortcake Funko POP #133	15
Strawberry Shortcake Orange Blossom Funko POP #134	40
Strawberry Shortcake Funko POP #135	23
Strawberry Shortcake DORBZ Blueberry Muffin #261	5

www.ingramcontent.com/pod-product-compliance
Lightning Source LLC
Chambersburg PA
CBHW052223150726

48002CB00003B/1256